Baybayin.com

An Introduction to B

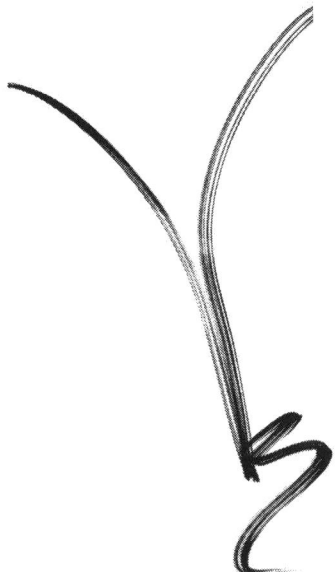

Baybayin.com | BaybayinBook.com | BaybayinSchool.com

All rights reserved. No part of this book may be reproduced or used in any way without the written permission except for reviews or articles. The title, author and website (Baybayin.com), must be credited. Salamat

Christian Cabuay
info@baybayin.com

Copyright © 2009

Baybayin.com

Dedicated
PNX & JZCA

Salamat
Family
Ray Haguisan
Paul Morrow
Christine Balza
Aleks Figueroa
Mitzi Duque-Ruiz PR
Know Your Roots
Pinoy Street Team
Filipino American Arts Exposition
Indian co-workers
Facebook & Twitter crew
Everyone I missed

Baybayin.com

Contents
Baybayin Chart – 1
Past & Present – 2
The Basics – 7
The Kudlit – 8
The Direction – 9
Writing Baybayin – 10
Modified Baybayin – 11
Writing your Name – 15
Sample Words – 18
Online Translators – 19
The Strokes – 20
The 17 Characters – 24
Baybayin Worksheet – 41
Thoughts – 42
Links – 43

CHRISTIAN CABUAY
BAYBAYIN.COM

A	E/I	O/U	
BA	B-E/I	B-O/U	B
KA	K-E/I	K-O/U	K
DA/RA	D/R-E/I	D/R-O/U	D/R
GA	G-E/I	G-O/U	G
HA	H-E/I	H-O/U	H
LA	L-E/I	L-O/U	L
MA	M-E/I	M-O/U	M
NA	N-E/I	N-O/U	N
NGA	NG-E/I	NG-O/U	NG
PA	P-E/I	P-O/U	P
SA	S-E/I	S-O/U	S
TA	T-E/I	T-O/U	T
WA	W-E/I	W-O/U	W
YA	Y-E/I	Y-O/U	Y

Isn't this Alibata? What's the difference? There is no difference between Alibata and Baybayin except that the name Alibata is incorrect. Alibata was a term coined by Professor Paul Versoza in the early 1900's. I once thought that he made the mistake of originating the script with Arabic until I read his book "Pangbansang Titik nang Pilipinas" 1939. You might have read the Versoza quote that's been re-quoted over and over again from Paul Morrow's site (mts.net/~pmorrow):

> In 1921 I returned from the United States to give public lectures on Tagalog philology, calligraphy, and linguistics. I introduced the word alibata, which found its way into newsprints and often mentioned by many authors in their writings. I coined this word in 1914 in the New York Public Library, Manuscript Research Division, basing it on the Maguindanao (Moro) arrangement of letters of the alphabet after the Arabic: alif, ba, ta (alibata), "f" having been eliminated for euphony's sake."

While that quote is accurate, it doesn't tell the whole story as to why he made-up the term. There wasn't any explanation why he linked the script to Arabic but there were some interesting points that may give you an idea of his motive. He writes about the origin of the word "Alphabet" and his seemingly admiration of other cultures who have names of their alphabet.

> The Japanese call theirs the KANA and HIRAGANA SYLLABARIES invented by a Buddhist monk in 700 AD which are based on the simple Chinese symbols. The Hindus call their Sanskrit alphabet DEVANGARI meaning "THE CITY OF GOD." (Pangbansang Titik nang Pilipinas pg 11 – Paul R. Verzosa – 1939)

The first characters in the Arabic alphabet are ALIF-BA-TA. The "F" was dropped due to it rolling off the tongue better as Alibata rather than Alifbata. Baybayin comes from the root word Baybay meaning to spell. Baybayin literally means, "To spell".

Maybe one of his goals to rename the script was to uplift it. He does acknowledge that the writing was indeed called Baybayin by the natives.

> *The first Spanish conquistadores and missionaries who came to the Philippines after the death of Magellan in the Island of Mactan found that the Tagalogs used to write their spoken speech in their native system called BAYBAYIN, and equivalent of Alphabet; but the literal meaning of Baybayin is TO SPELL OUT or SYLLABICATE.(Pangbansang Titik nang Pilipinas pg 11 – Paul R. Verzosa – 1939)*

It looks like he wasn't content with the generic term of Baybayin literally meaning to spell. Perhaps he wanted something more majestic in order to give the Filipinos a sense of pride. He does document that Baybayin is a direct descendant of Sanskrit.

> *Asia adopted the various simplified and popularized Sanskrit alphabet and handwriting, of which the Tagalog handwriting is its distant but direct descendant.(Pangbansang Titik nang Pilipinas pg 17 – Paul R. Verzosa – 1939)*

The origins of the script can be traced back to India just like most languages and writing systems in South-East Asia.

Two Filipino scholars, Tavera and Paterno, have concluded that about 25% of the Philippine vocabularies can be traced to Indian influence. (HinduWisdom.info)

Some examples of common Tagalog and Indian words:

English	Tagalog	Indian
Poverty	Dukha	Dukha
Teacher	Guro	Guru
Faith	Sampalataya	Sampratyaya
Face	Mukha	Mukha
Eclipse	Laho	Rahu
Cat	Pusa	Pucha (Malayalam)
Story	Katha	Katha

Usage

Baybayin was used to write short notes such as poetry and announcements. History wasn't recorded in the script. It was carved in natural material such as bamboo.

Death

One popular train of thought on the demise of the script is to blame the Spanish. While it's easy to blame everything on them, we probably have most our information about the script thanks to the Spanish. With the double-edged sword of knowledge preservation and cultural eradication, they helped keep the script alive by putting it in books and sending them abroad for safekeeping. The very first book printed (up for debate) in the Philippines contained Baybayin. The Doctrina Christiana was published in 1593 as a tool to confirm the natives to Christianity. It worked.

There weren't any mass burnings of any Baybayin manuscripts. The fact that we wrote on organic material such as bamboo severely shortened the lifespan of the writings.

What probably happened was what occurs when a new generation wants to make money. The fact was that we were colonized. In order to adapt to this new society, one had to learn new skills to survive. One of them was a new writing system. Times were changing and the standards for literacy were different. Think of it like a generation that used the typewriter then needed to adapt to the new environment of computers. People wanted the new material goods (and illusion of power) that the Spanish brought in. The best way to get it was through money. Money comes from jobs and jobs come from knowledge. Know how to read and write using the new writing system? You would have a better chance of earning a living. It's still like that today. Don't know English or how to write English? Pretty soon it will be "You need to know Chinese" to get this job or you probably will not make as much money as the next person who does know this new skill. There's a reason why the call-center industry boomed in the Philippines – English. So, one can argue that Baybayin died a natural death.

Baybayin now
On the flipside, if the Spanish never came and others did not colonize us, we probably would either be writing a mutated version of Baybayin or Arabic or a combination of the two. There are people who wonder why we don't revive and use Baybayin today. In order to do so the writing system would have been expanded and modified to adapt to new sounds brought in naturally from the modern world.

Today, the script has penetrated the psyche of Fil-ams by way of tattoos. Without the tattoo movement, there most likely wouldn't be much interest in it. Right behind tattoos is Filipino themed apparel. There are numerous Filipino shirt companies, mostly created by Filipino-Americans who use the script (sometimes incorrectly) in their clothing lines to represent their version of so-called Pinoy Pride. Filipinos are also in style thanks to international celebrities such as Manny Pacquiao, Apl.de.ap, Nicole Scherzinger, HappySlip, JabbaWockeeZ, and Brandon Vera who sports more than a few Baybayin tattoos.

Another reason for this resurgence is the internet. With highly informative sites by Hector Santos, Paul Morrow and even Wikipedia, the generation of today has quick and easy access to the Baybayin.

There are also a few people who've made Baybayin into an art form by stylizing the basic characters into their own creative way through graffiti, jewelry, digital art, and tattoos.

In the Philippines, there are still a few tribes that use a mutated version of Baybayin. These would be the Buhids, Hanunoos and Tagbanwan. For more information, please visit bibingka.com/dahon/living/living.htm.

Basics

Baybayin is an abugida writing system consisting of 14 consonants and 3 vowels. Each of the 14 consonants ends with the vowel "A". For example, the letter B would be BA. The Thai, Balinese, and Sanskrit scripts also have similar characteristics.

The original alphabet consists of the following characters:

Vowels
A, E/I, O/U

Consonants
Ba, Ka, Da, Ga, Ha, La, Ma, Na, Nga, Pa, Sa, Ta, Wa, Ya

The E/I and O/U sounds share the same character making it a challenge to read. The Da character is also interchangeable with the Ra sound as in Ma**D**ami/Ma**R**ami or ako **D**in/ako **R**in. The La character can also be interchanged with Da. Non-"Filipino" words could also use the La opposed to the Da/Ra, although that was inconsistent.

Kudlit
The kudlit is a small mark above or below a consonant character to change the pronunciation properties.

The Ka character alone looks like this:

With the kudlit above it would be either Ke or Ki.

A kudlit below the character would be either Ko or Ku.

In traditional Baybayin, you wouldn't use kudlits for vowels.

Punctuation
Generally, a vertical line was used like a comma or a break in a sentence much like what we use in English. A double vertical line represented a period. Each writer used these punctuation marks at their own discretion.

kalayaan at kapayapaan
(freedom and peace)

Direction

There have been a few ideas as to what direction the script was actually written in. One way of "writing" Baybayin was to carve the characters into bamboo with a dagger. In order not to cut themselves, the writer would start from the bottom up with the top of the characters to the left as illustrated below.

When written on paper or leaves, it was from left to right. However, it seems that the script was also written in multiple directions depending on the writer. Besides the "missing" characters, this was another reason why the Spanish tried to modify the script.

Writing Baybayin

Baybayin is actually easy to learn if you follow the 2 basic rules.

1) Consonants and vowels – Each of the consonant characters is pronounced with an "A" at the end. If you wanted to write Cavite, it would be Ka-Bi-Te not C-A-V-I-T-E.

Correct

Cavite (Ka-Bi-Te)

Incorrect

Ka-A-Ba-I-Ta-E

2) Kudlit – In order to transform the trailing vowel "A" to an E/I or O/U, you would make a small mark above the character for E/I or below it for an O/U.

That's pretty much it. Traditional Baybayin works best with Filipino words (not just Tagalog but other dialects as well) or words that follow the same pronunciation pattern. You will run into problems trying to make a literal translation of John Smith using traditional Baybayin. It also helps a lot if you speak and know the proper Tagalog pronunciation. As long as you spell as it's pronounced, you should be good.

Modified Baybayin

There have been a few attempts to alter the original Baybayin for modern use. The first attempt to "reform" the script was in 1620 when Fr. Francisco Lopez was about to publish the Ilokano Doctrina. Seeing the "limitations" of Baybayin, he invented a new kudlit in the shape of a cross +. When placed under a consonant, it would cancel the "a" vowel.

I personally don't like it due to the colonial origins and overall artistic look but I do see the purpose of it, putting my cultural preference aside. If you look at Baybayin as purely a writing system, this modification is a natural process. Thanks to the renewed interest of Baybayin, the Spanish kudlit has made a comeback due people wanting a "complete" translation. Some find it difficult to accept "missing" characters, especially if its going to be a tattoo.

I use an X as it has more of a canceling property compared to the + sign. Besides the X or +, some modernized Baybayin alphabets use cancellation kudlits above and below the characters for extra sound properties. In my artwork, I've incorporated the cancellation kudlit in the character.

One common Baybayin tattoo is the Tagalog word for STRENGTH – LAKAS. Using traditional Baybayin, it would be written without the SA character because of the missing vowel.

La   Ka   S

Using the Spanish cancellation kudlit, it would look like this with the Sa character modified.

La   Ka   S

Modern Baybayin

There have been a few radical attempts to modernize Baybayin for usage today. They include extra characters not in the original alphabet as well as new kudlit techniques separating the E, I, O, and U vowels. Some modernists are Bayani Mendoza de Leon, Nordex, and Frederick Victor Paredes Añana.

Aklatin Heavy by Frederick Victor Paredes Añana
aklatinheavy.blogspot.com

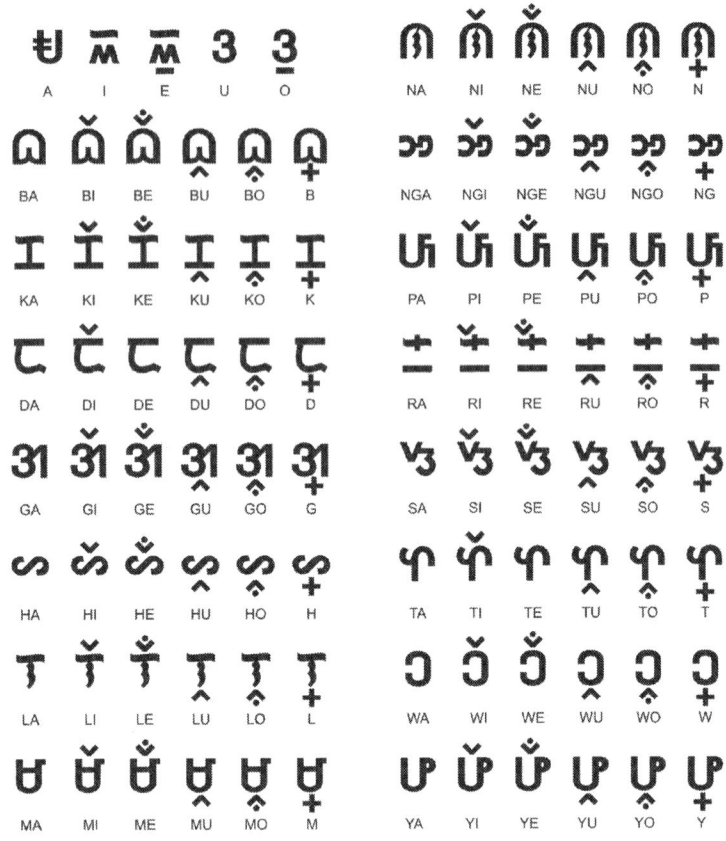

Baybayin.com

Aklatin Heavy by Frederick Victor Paredes Añana
aklatinheavy.blogspot.com

OTHER CONSONANTS

PUNCTUATION MARKS

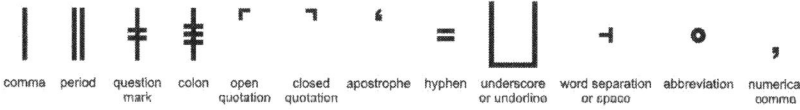

NUMERALS

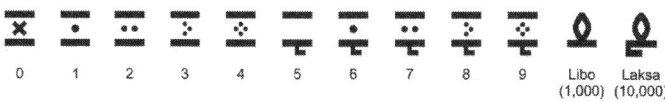

MATHEMATICAL SYMBOLS

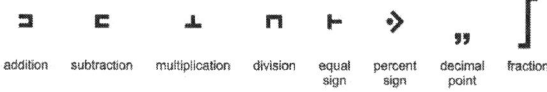

Names
The general Baybayin rule is to spell as pronounced and drop off anything without a vowel after it, but names can break those rules. Since people pronounce their names differently, it's entirely up to you how you want it translated to Baybayin. Some traditional translation examples:

Rhea = De/Re-Ya
I assume it's pronounced ReYa but if you say ReA then the translation would be De/Re-A. The H isn't pronounced and is dropped.

Re Ya

Aguila = A-Gi-La
If you don't pronounce the U, then drop it. If you pronounce it, then the translation would be A-GU-I-LA.

A   Gi   La

A   Gu   I   La

Now for some "difficult" names

Cruz = Ka-Du/Ru
Traditional Baybayin rules tells us that only 1 character should be written (Du). To get the sound of Cruz, it could be done like this.

Ku Ru

Anastasia = A-Na-Ta-Si-Ya
Just like Rhea, I assume it's pronounced YA at the end. It can be done a couple ways.

A   Na   Ta   Si   Ya

A   Na   Sa   Ta   Si   Ya

Junior = DI-YO-NI-YO
Since there's no J in Baybayin, a combo of the Da & Ya characters with kuldits do the trick of emulating the J sound.

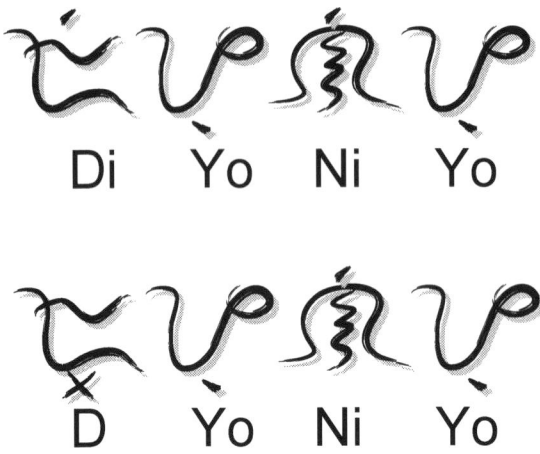

Christian = KA-DI/RI-TI-YA
My name can be done several ways.

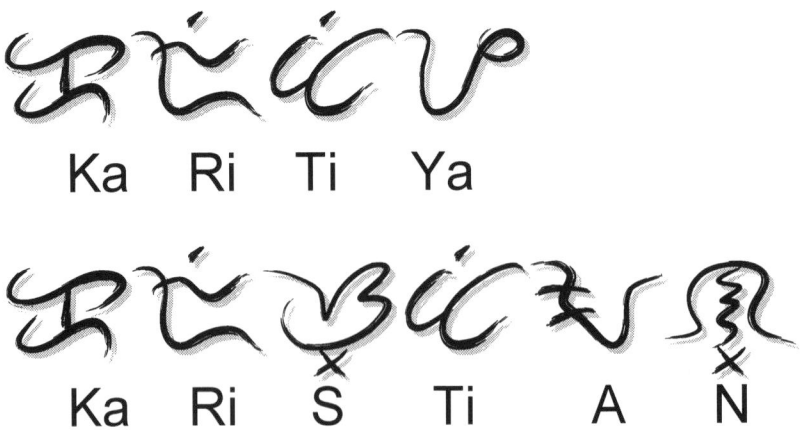

Baybayin examples
Lakas | Strength

Kalayaan | Freedom

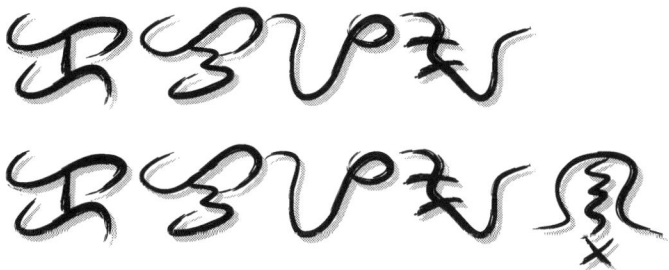

Maganda | Beautiful

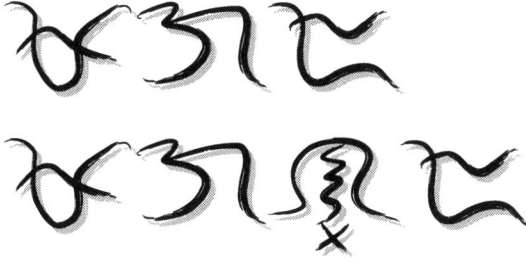

Filipino

Translators

There are a few online translators out there that will convert the entered text to Baybayin characters. The most popular one is known as "Eagles Corner" by Victor Quimson. While these programs seem easy to use and pretty accurate, they are only good as what you put into them. Garbage in, garbage out. These programs lack context. They do not know the difference between names and words. They also cannot translate based on pronunciation. For example, if you type "Maria", the output would be Ma-Di-A. While it may seem right in a literal sense, the output should be Ma-Di-Ya as its pronounced as Mariya.

Another common mistake is that some people think it's an English to Tagalog or any other Filipino language translator. I saw a tattoo that read Si-Te that was supposed to mean Ate. What the person probably did was type "Sister" in an online translator.

Strokes

One of the most difficult things in Baybayin is getting used to the way the strokes are written. Most of the 17 characters can be easily mastered if you practice these 4 basic strokes. Please note that these exercises are based on my personal Baybayin writing style. Each person will write it differently. Use this method but develop your own personal style overtime.

This stroke can be seen in La, Ka and Ha.

Baybayin.com

This stroke can be seen in O/U, Ga, La, Sa and Nga.

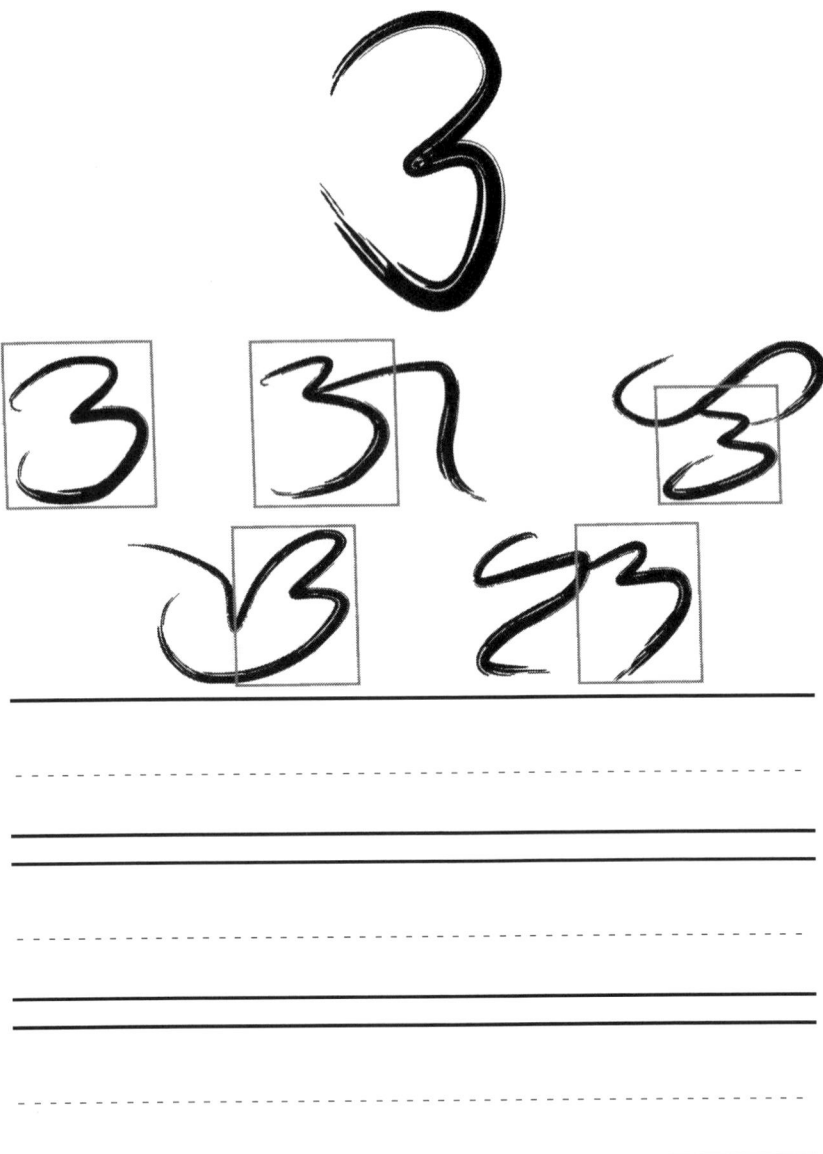

This stroke can be seen in Ya, Pa, A, Ma, Sa, Wa.

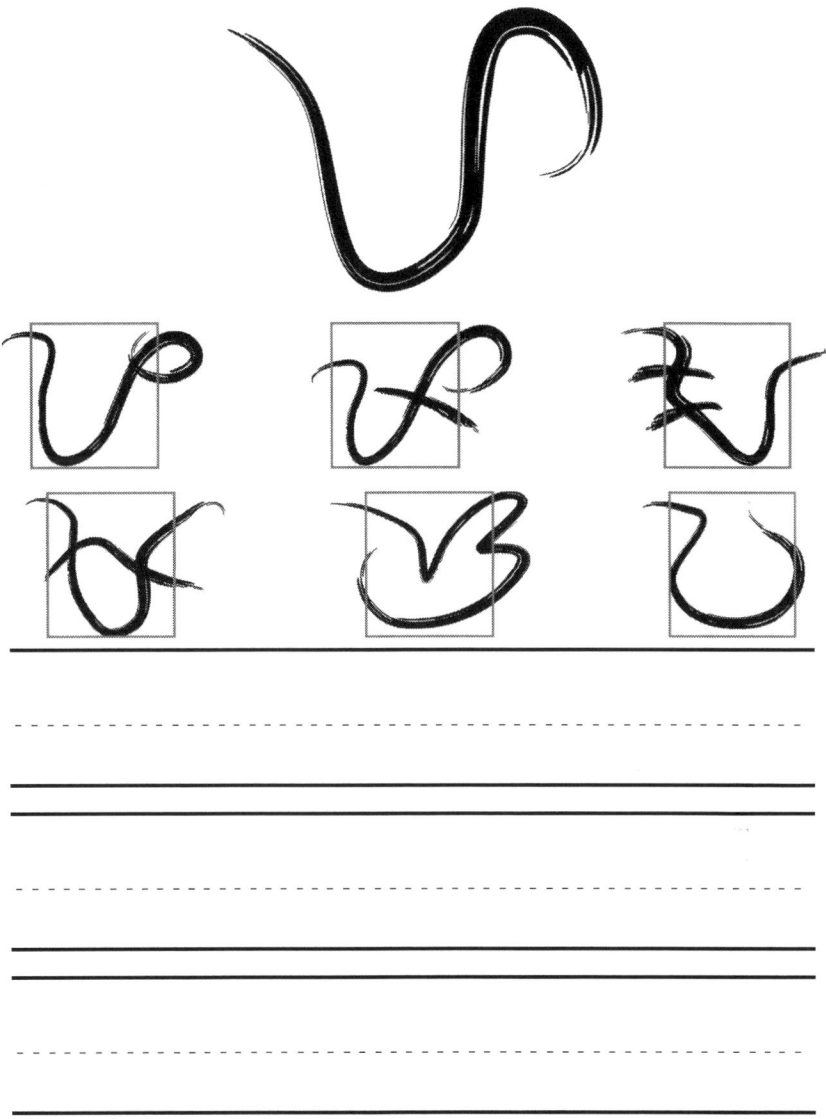

This stroke can be seen in E/I, La and Na.

Baybayin.com

Writing the characters

A

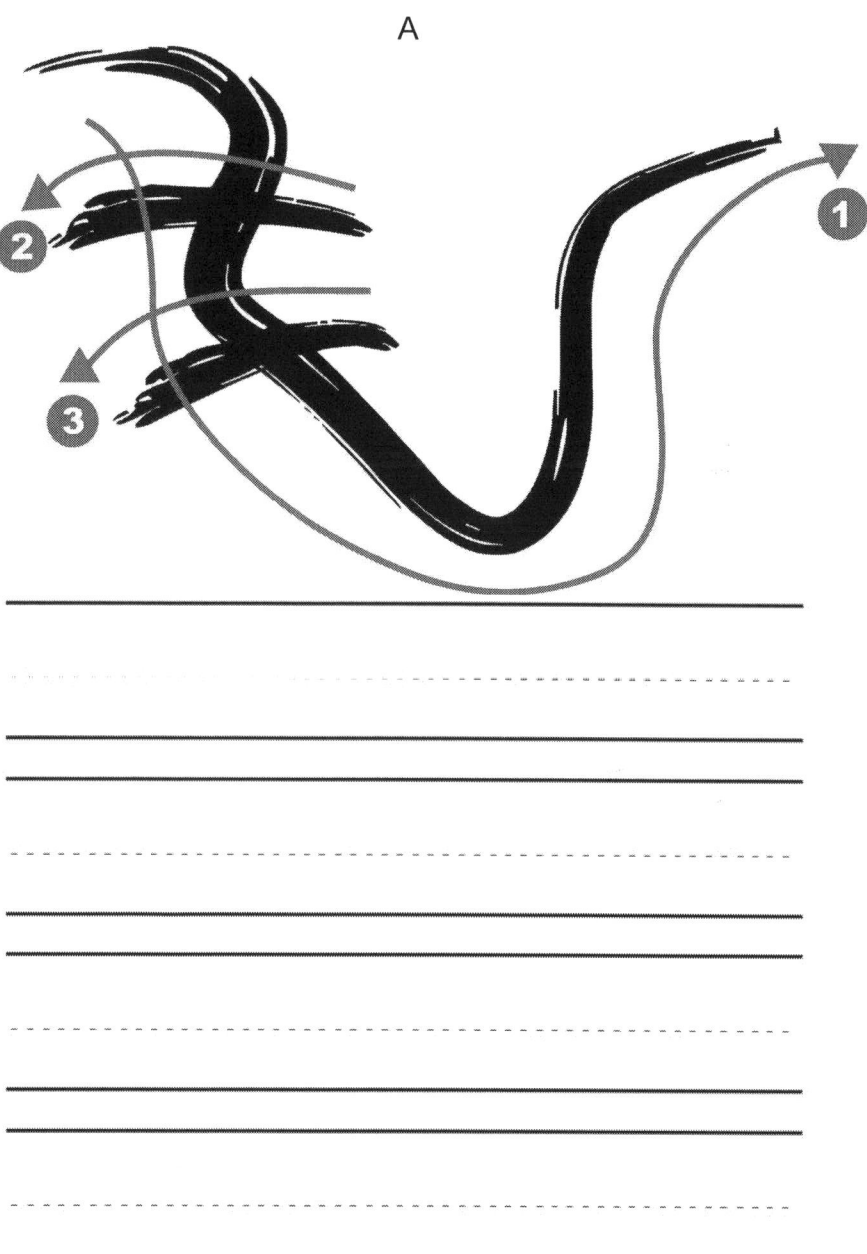

E/I

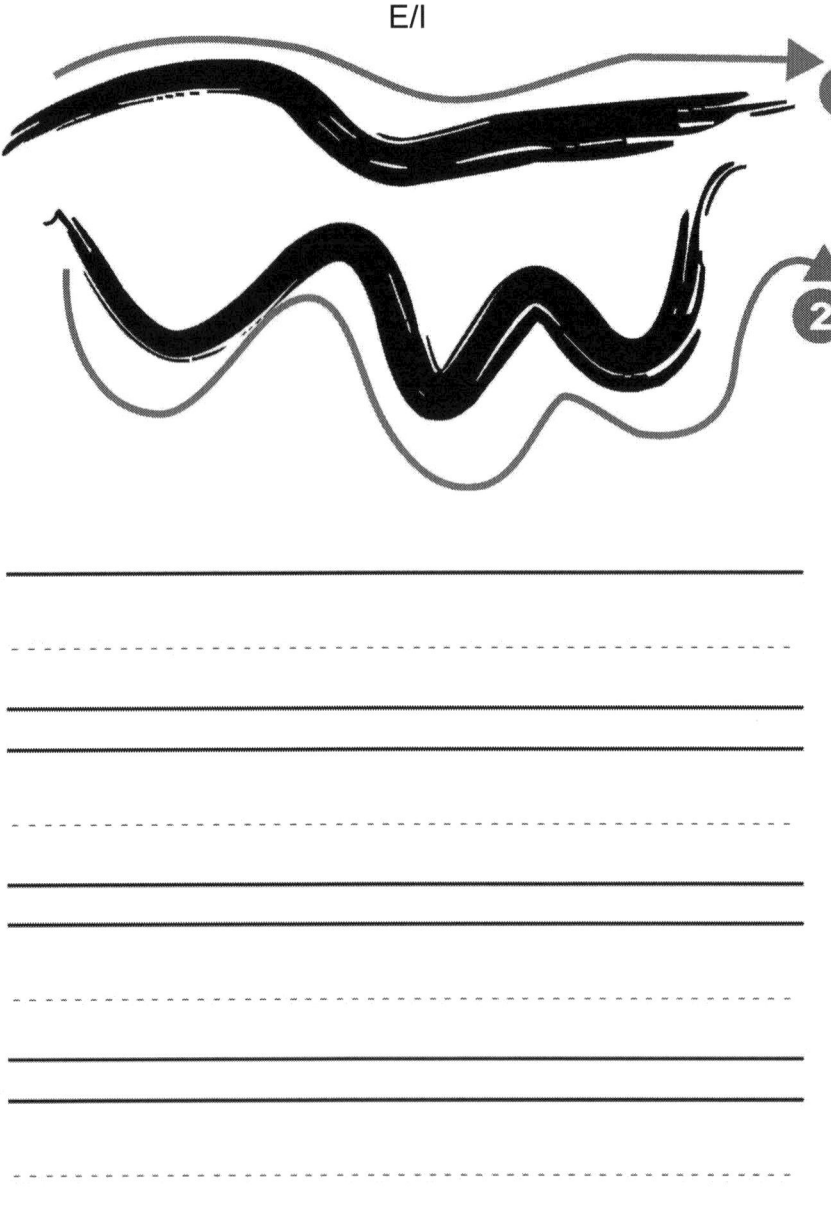

O/U

Ba

Ka

Da

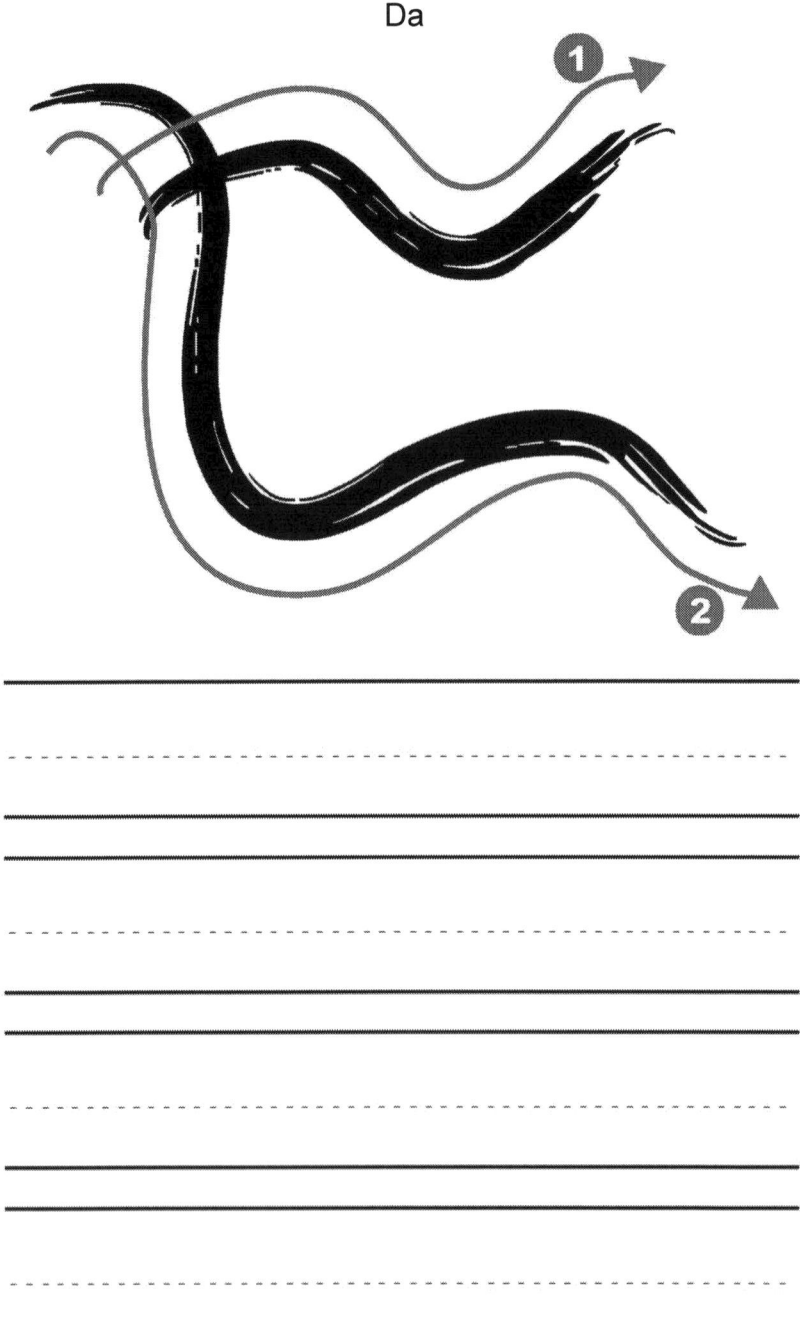

Baybayin.com

Ga

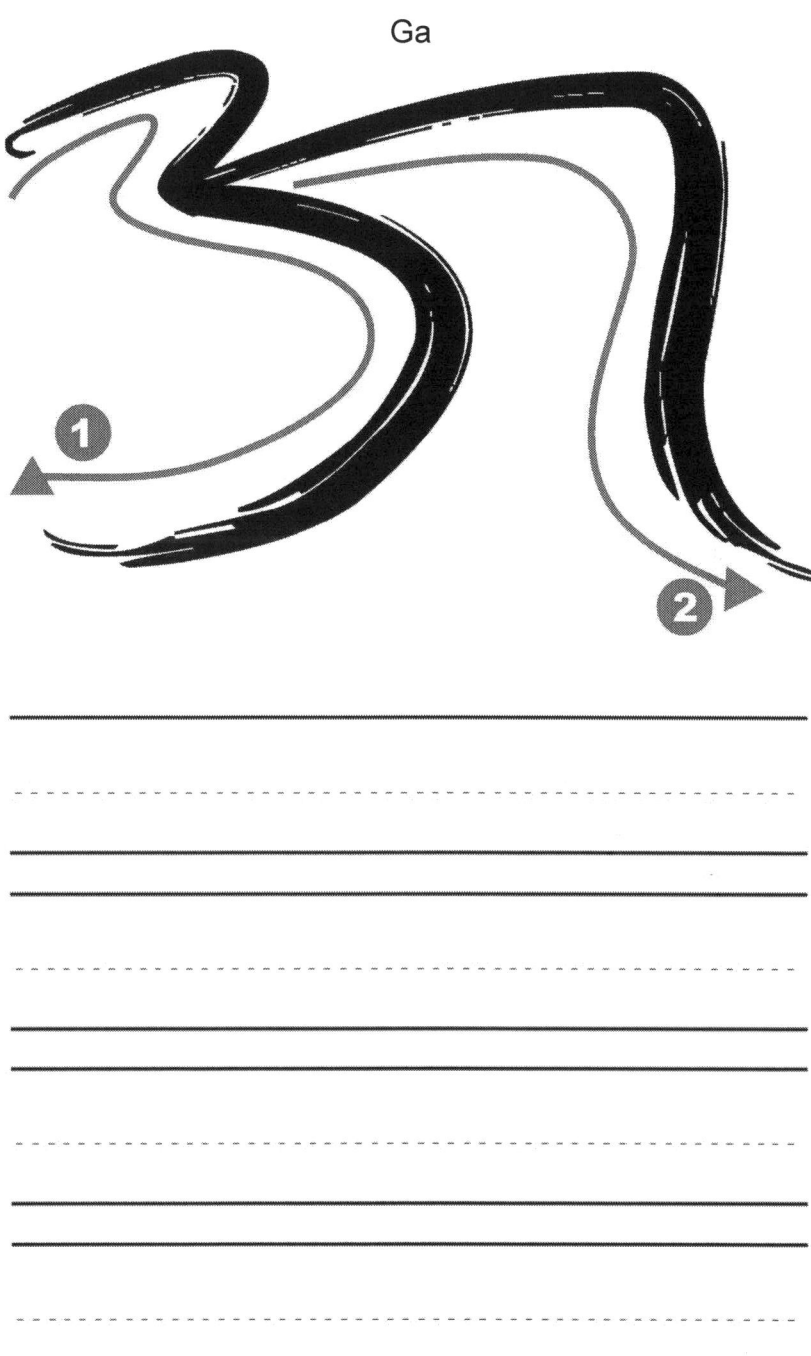

Ha

La

Baybayin.com

Ma

Baybayin.com

Na

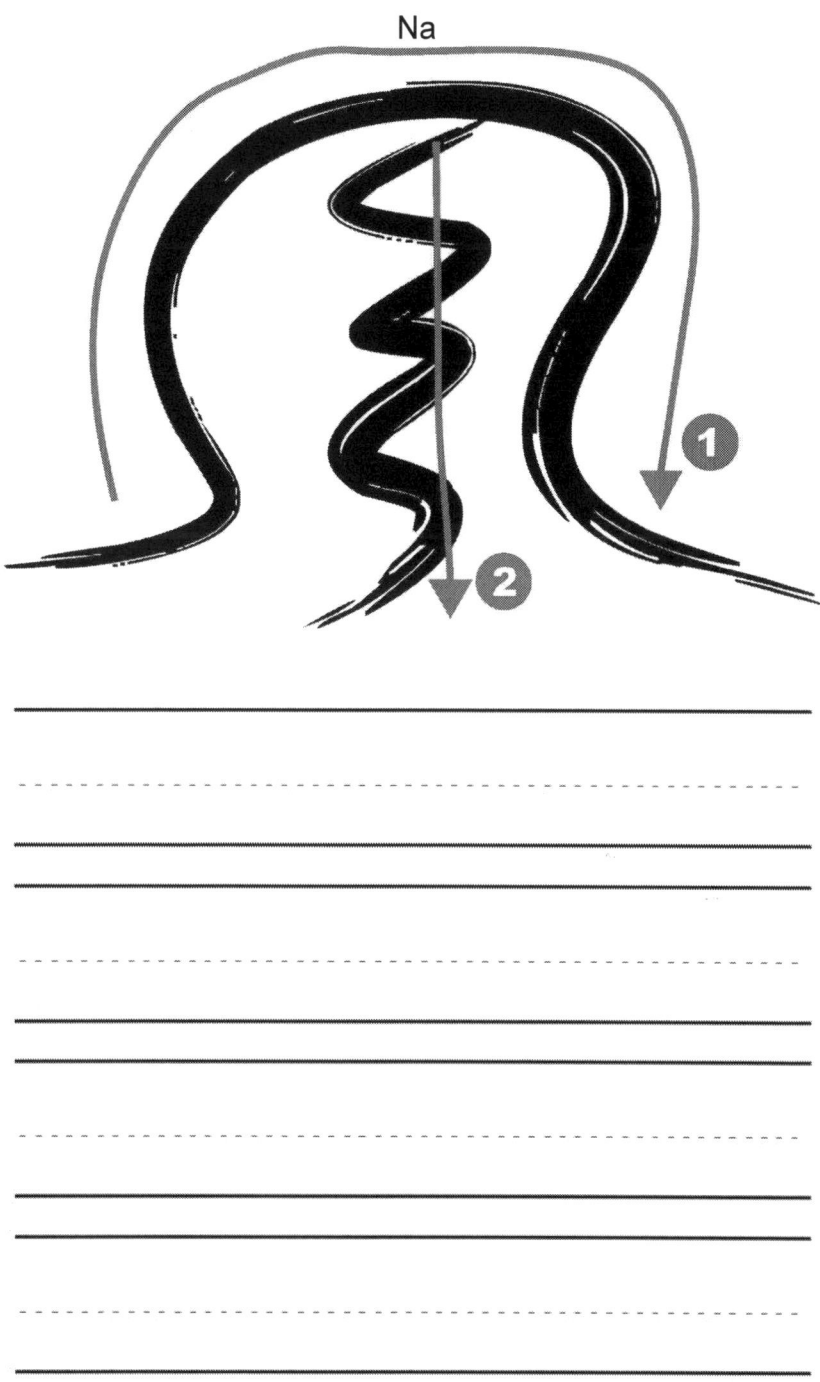

Nga

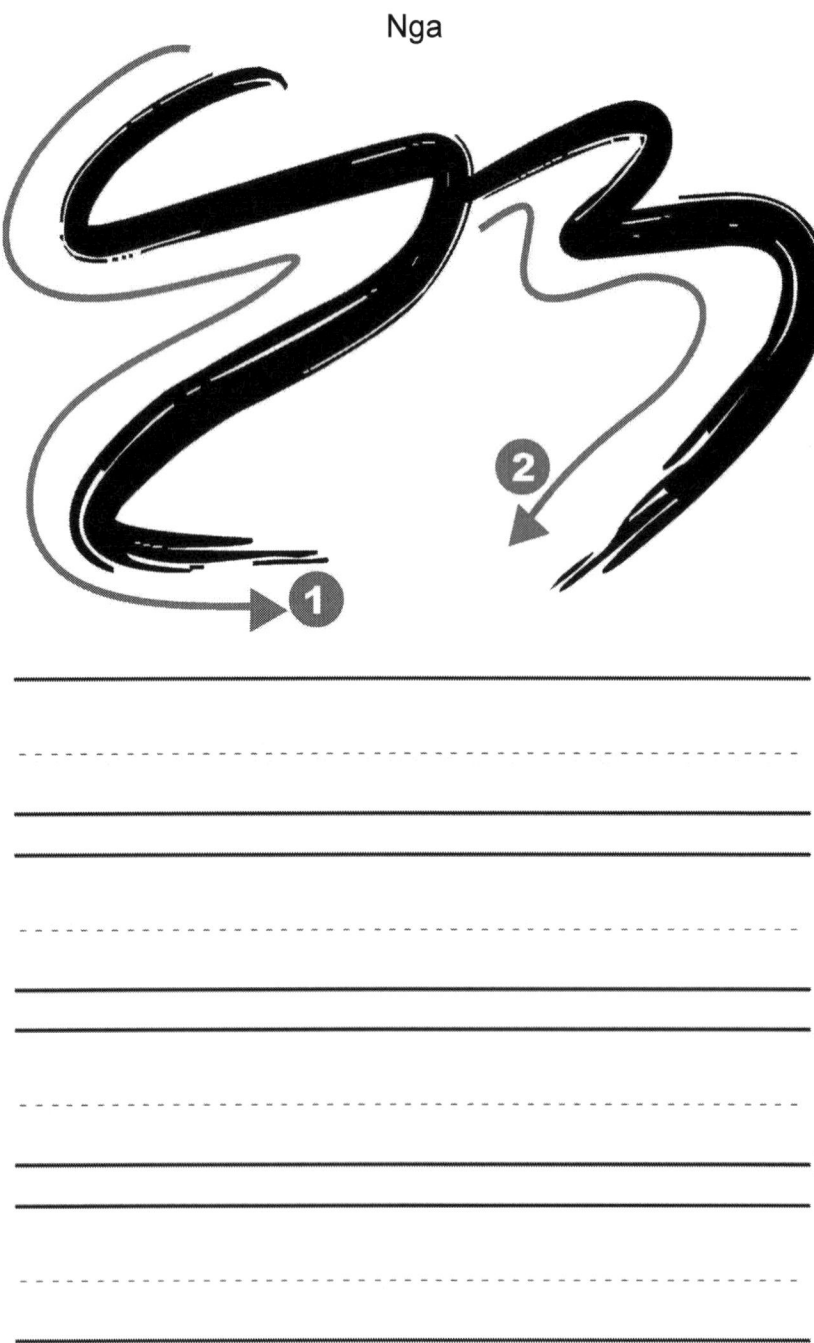

Baybayin.com

Pa

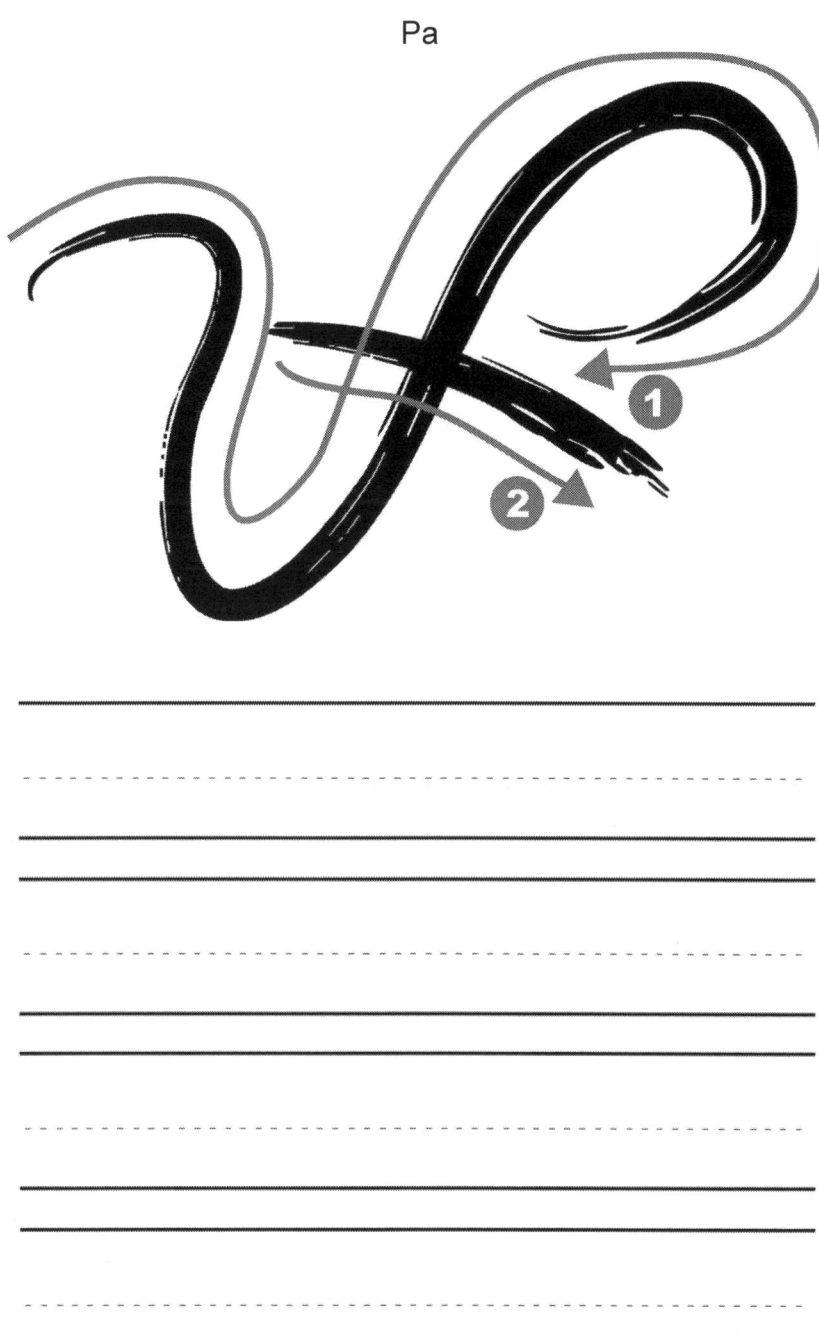

Sa

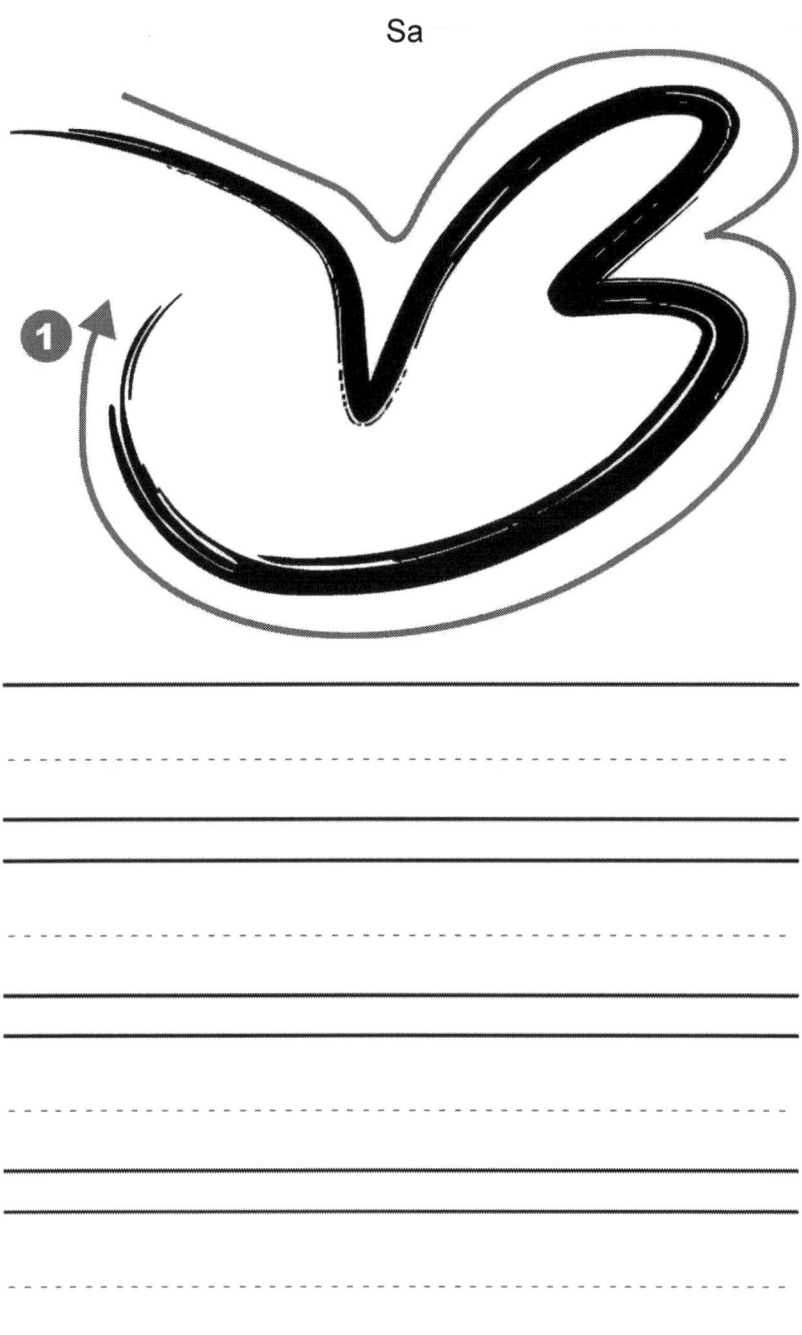

Ta

Wa

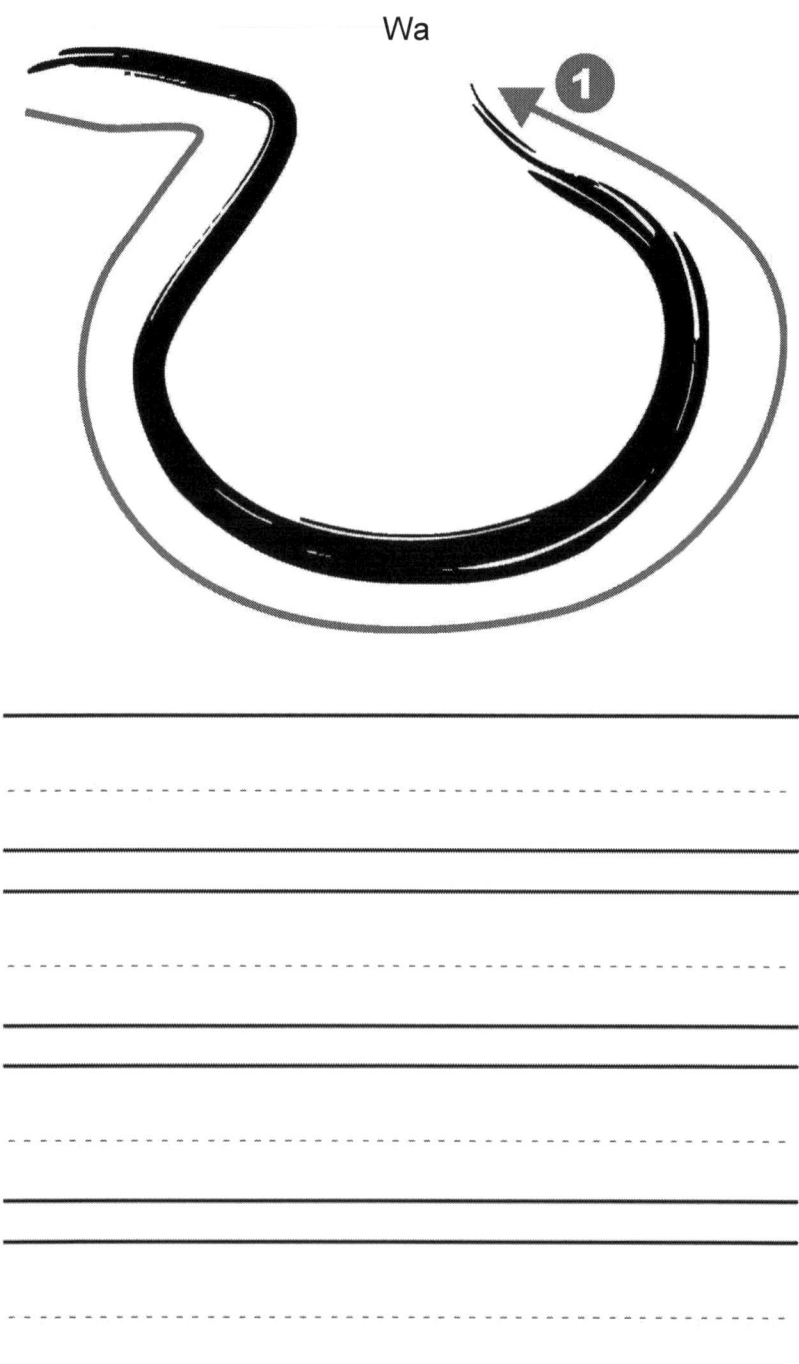

Ya

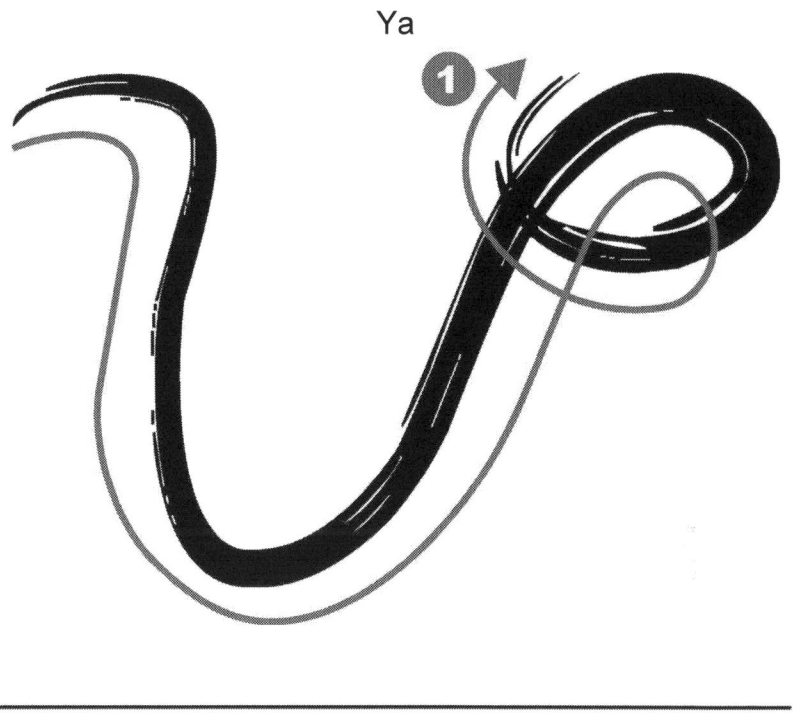

Baybayin.com

Download more practice worksheets at BAYBAYIN.com

A	E/I	O/U
꜊	꜊	꜊

BA	B-E/I	B-O/U	B
꜊	꜊	꜊	꜊

KA	K-E/I	K-O/U	K
꜊	꜊	꜊	꜊

DA/RA	D/R-E/I	D/R-O/U	D/R
꜊	꜊	꜊	꜊

GA	G-E/I	G-O/U	G
꜊	꜊	꜊	꜊

HA	H-E/I	H-O/U	H
꜊	꜊	꜊	꜊

LA	L-E/I	L-O/U	L
꜊	꜊	꜊	꜊

MA	M-E/I	M-O/U	M
꜊	꜊	꜊	꜊

NA	N-E/I	N-O/U	N
꜊	꜊	꜊	꜊

NGA	NG-E/I	NG-O/U	NG
꜊	꜊	꜊	꜊

PA	P-E/I	P-O/U	P
꜊	꜊	꜊	꜊

SA	S-E/I	S-O/U	S
꜊	꜊	꜊	꜊

TA	T-E/I	T-O/U	T
꜊	꜊	꜊	꜊

WA	W-E/I	W-O/U	W
꜊	꜊	꜊	꜊

YA	Y-E/I	Y-O/U	Y
꜊	꜊	꜊	꜊

Copyright © 2008 Baybayin.com | info@baybayin.com

Thoughts

There's nothing mystical about the script. No deep secrets to unlock hidden messages. Ultimately, we put meaning into it to it. Getting the basics down is the easy part. Getting historical and social context is where it gets tricky. Once you know the basic rules, experiment and develop your own style.

Use this manual as your Baybayin starting point, but I urge you to dig deeper into pre-Filipino culture. While this is only a simple writing system that was prematurely lost, its roots will open your mind and will help you realize where we really came from. It is my wish that you uncover what we were before colonization and act on it.

Christian Cabuay

Baybayin links

Paul Morrow – One of the most in-depth sites on Baybayin
mts.net/~pmorrow
Hector Santos – One of the most in-depth sites on Baybayin
bibingka.com/dahon/tagalog/tagalog.htm
Aleks Figueroa – Neo-tribal Filipino tattoo art
FilipinoTattoos.com
Ray Haguisan – The original Baybayin wood burner
MalayaDesigns.net
Christine Balza – Baybayin jewelry
Suku-Art.com
Michelle Ruschman – Baybayin jewelry
PhilippineScriptDesigns.com
Online Baybayin translator
eaglescorner.com/baybayin/baybayin.html
Graffiti inspired Baybayin art
TheBathalaProject.com
Anak Bathala Project - Modern Baybayin fonts
nordenx.blogspot.com
Baybayin iPhone app
GastonSantiago.com
Omniglot – Writing systems and Languages of the world
Omniglot.com
Mary Ann Ubaldo – Baybayin jeweler and Filipino spiritualist
Urduja.com
Frederick Victor Paredes Añana – Modern Baybayin fonts
fredsbaybayintopics.blogspot.com

Other links
MitziDuqueRuiz.com – PR Consultant
HinduWisdom.info – India & the Philippines

See Baybayin.com/links for a living list

My websites

All about Baybayin
Baybayin.com
Baybayin community
Baybayin.org
Online Baybayin course
BaybayinSchool.com
Baybayin books
BaybayinBook.com
My personal Facebook page
Facebook.com/Baybayin
Follow Baybayin!
Twitter.com/Baybayin
The Filipino Tattoo Source with Baybayin art services
PinoyTattoos.com
Filipino Tattoo Facebook page
Facebook.com/PinoyTattoos
Follow PinoyTattoos!
Twitter.com/PinoyTattoos
Filipino Street Fashion
PinoyStreetWear.com
One man business ramblings
LivingroomCEO.com

Need more worksheets? Get more at Baybayin.com
Feel free to reach out with any questions or inquiries.

Printed in Great Britain
by Amazon